▌ PRIVATE EYE

Mediaballs
2

**All the world's best
media rubbish, including:**

- ● **The stupidest quiz show answers**
- ● **The worst misprints**
- ● **The most pretentious writers**
- ● **The silliest actors**

Edited by **Marcus Berkmann**

Illustrated by **Grizelda**

The Southern Reporter

CAPTION CAPTION: about these pious little bleeders and the lady busser doing that interminably boring thing so cherished by Border festivals. What on earth is going on in this picture – these people have got to get out more often.

Published in Great Britain
by Private Eye Productions Ltd,
6 Carlisle Street, London W1D 3BN

©2005 Pressdram Ltd
ISBN 1 901784 40 1
Designed by Bridget Tisdall
Printed in England by
Clays Ltd, St Ives plc

DUMB BRITAIN

Real contestants, real quiz shows, real answers, real dumb

Anne Robinson: Name the doctor who founded children's homes and orphanages in Britain in the late 19th century.
Contestant: Dr Dolittle.

The Weakest Link

Jeff Owen: In which country is Mount Everest?
Contestant *(long pause)***:** Er, it's not in Scotland is it?
Jeff Owen: Which classical composer became deaf in later life: Ludvig van...?
Same contestant *(immediate answer)***:** Van Gogh.

BBC Radio Nottingham

Melanie Sykes: In which city is the world-famous Raffles Hotel?
Contestant: Is it Birmingham?

The Vault

Anne Robinson: What 'R' is the westernmost island of the British Isles?
Contestant: Argyll.

The Weakest Link

Anne Robinson: Vietnam has land borders with Laos and Cambodia and which other country?
Contestant *(after long pause)*: America.

The Weakest Link

Presenter: Where is the Sea of Tranquillity?
Contestant: Weston-super-Mare.

Get Your Own Back, BBC Prime

Anne Robinson: What item of photographic equipment has the same name as the private chamber of a judge?
Contestant: Tripod.

The Weakest Link

Anne Robinson: Which activity, which can be primary, secondary, higher, further or adult, is mainly conducted in schools or universities?
Contestant: Pass.

The Weakest Link

Melanie Sykes: What is the name given to the condition where the sufferer can fall asleep at any time?
Contestant: Nostalgic.

The Vault

Anne Robinson: In the City of London, the Monument commemorates which 17th-century event?
Contestant: Er... the First World War?

The Weakest Link

James Cannon: Which of these actors did NOT star in a Carry On film: Sid James, Kenneth Williams, Hattie Jacques or Laurence Olivier?
Contestant: Hattie Jacques.

Capital FM early show

Presenter: What was the name of Queen Victoria's husband?
Teenage girl: Dirty Den.

The Saturday Show, BBC1

Anne Robinson: Which month in the Gregorian calendar is named after Augustus Caesar?
Contestant: June.

The Weakest Link

Melanie Sykes: In the Bible, which disciple betrayed Jesus?
Contestant: Solomon.

The Vault

Nick Knowles: What was the name of Bill and Hillary Clinton's cat?
Contestant: Was it Monica?

Judgemental, BBC1

Paul Ross: In which county would you find Wentworth golf course?
Contestant: I'll have to say Wentworth because I don't know any counties.

No Win No Fee, BBC1

Jeff Owen: Where did the D-Day landings take place?
Contestant (*after pause*): Pearl Harbour?

BBC Radio Nottingham

Alex Trelinski: What is the capital of Italy?
Contestant: France.
Trelinski: France is another country. Try again.
Contestant: Oh, um, Benidorm.
Trelinski: Wrong, sorry, let's try another question.
In which country is the Parthenon?
Same contestant: Sorry, I don't know.
Trelinski: Just guess a country then.
Contestant: Paris.

BBC Midlands

Anne Robinson: What 'Z' is used to describe a
human who has returned from the dead?
Contestant: Unicorn.

The Weakest Link

Contestant: It stands in a field and it shouts "moo".
Richard Madeley: A sheep.

'You Say We Pay', *Richard And Judy*, C4

■ Former football legend . . .
George Bush and his wife Alex

Swindon Evening Advertiser

Mr Winsor's other missive yesterday was an attempt to put the brakes on Notwork Rail, whose annual spending he wants down from £6 billion to £4 billion within five years.

Daily Telegraph

Le prince Charles et Camilla Parker Bowels à une soirée de gala sur Shakespeare à Londres

Photo caption, Var-Matin (Toulouse)

1900 Austin Powers - The Spy Who Shagged the Spy Who Shagged Me

Sunday Times of India

THE CEYLON Place Baptist Church has been sold — but the congregation are still searching for someone to worship.

Eastbourne Herald

THE NEOPHILIACS

"Coat hangers are the new rock 'n' roll."
Elle Decoration

"Allotments really are the new rock 'n' roll."
Western Mail

"Chicken-keeping is the new rock 'n' roll."
Northern Echo

"It's official. Cooking is the new rock 'n' roll."
Daily Record

"Going to the gym is the new rock 'n' roll."
Evening Standard

"Knitting... it's practically the new rock 'n' roll."
Sunday Express

"The second world war is clearly the new rock 'n' roll."
Sunday Times

"Modesty is the new rock 'n' roll."
Jess Cartner-Morley, *The Guardian*

"Modesty's the new black."

Independent On Sunday

"Red is the new black."

Sunday Times

" 'Green is the new black,' says funeral director."

Leicester Mercury

"Next season, individuality is the new black."

The Observer

"Islamophobia is the new black."

The Observer

"Chrysanthemums are the new black."

Flower Council of Holland

"Stupid – it's the new black."

Sunday Times Style section

"Accountancy is the new black."

Accountancy magazine *PQ*

"Saris are the new shoulder pads."

Daily Telegraph

"Boots are the new shoes."

Sunday Times Style section

"Cardigans are the new jackets."
James Delingpole, *The Times*

"Tweed is the new black lycra."
Jess Cartner-Morley, *The Guardian*

"Armani declares demure the new daring."
Jess Cartner-Morley, *The Guardian*

"As sure as green is the new pink, so zhooshy is the new fabulous, the word used to convey style approval."
Jess Cartner-Morley, *The Guardian*

"Ankles, we are told, are soon to be the new breasts."
Editorial in *The Times*

"Nipples are the new cleavage."
Alison MacLeod, *Prospect*

"Giving birth is clearly the new adopting."
Scotland On Sunday

"Cockroaches are the new cats."
thisislondon.co.uk

"Wood is the new grass."
What's New in Building

"Red is the new green."
British Red Cross

"Green is the new red."
Peter Tatchell, *The Guardian*

"Blue is now the new green."
Waitrose Food Illustrated

"There's a shade of purple that's the new pink."
Sunday Times Style section

"Black is frequently the new black. But this season it isn't. It's purple."
Laura Craik, *Evening Standard*

Pseuds Corner

Pretentious media-related tripe from the Eye's most venerable column

The most surprising thing about the rehearsal is how Macy [Gray] keeps it together – ringmaster, not freakshow. She is so good at it that she lies down on one of the sofas and simultaneously sings, gives directions and reads a novel. She is both very present and in her own world. Watching her read her book and keep the beat, I realise that it is possible to coexist with humanity and be totally mentally divergent.

Emma Forrest, *Telegraph Magazine*

Geoff Dyer's books can have a strange effect on readers. A friend of mine to whom I lent *But Beautiful*, his extended essay on jazz musicians of the Forties and Fifties, ripped it in half. "Did you hate it?" I asked. "The opposite. It was too good. I couldn't bear to be in the presence of something that powerful." Another friend was so inflamed by reading *Out Of Sheer Rage*, Dyer's gloriously acidic anti-study of D.H. Lawrence, that she packed in her PhD and ran off to the mountains of Peru.

Sukhdev Sandhu, *Telegraph Magazine*

You will love and admire us and want to be our friends. We will inspire you because we are the future. You will learn from us. Come, take our hand. We are going to show you our world.

Invitation to Royal College of Art event

I had reached that point in life when one has published a novel or two...

Philip Hensher, *The Independent*

When he orders fish, he asks his purveyor to pack and transport the fish in the direction in which it was swimming when it was caught. One might easily laugh at this and ask why, but Keller's response would be to counter, why not? Why stress the flesh of the fish unnecessarily, if you don't have to?

Andrew Gumbel reviewing The French Laundry
Restaurant, California, *The Independent*

[Damon Albarn] is making up for being out of the limelight: eyes bulging, jaw locked, wringing with sweat, willing the crowd – in a faintly Nietzschean sense – to love the new stuff.

Kitty Empire, *Observer Review*

My new book has got paedophilia, September 11 and lots of black people in it. I'm moving on, we've got to progress.

Jilly Cooper speaking at the
Hay Literary festival, quoted in the *Guardian*

Marc Quinn is best known for Self (1991), a model of his head made from nine pints of his frozen blood, now on show at the Saatchi Gallery in County Hall, London. More recently, Quinn created a model of his four-day-old son's head, made from his girlfriend's liquidised placenta.

Guardian Weekend

But as ballsy belligerence gave way to millennial flakiness, so cleansing emerged as the cosmetic ceremony *du jour*, with its modish connotations of purifying, stripping bare and revealing the inner outer self. If moisturiser is the double espresso of the beauty world, then cleanser is its camomile tea... something I look forward to, a cathartic close to the end of the day. Besides, it's so now, so this time of year.

Hannah Betts, *The Times*

Every generation since the war has had its great pop cultural moment, thanks to teddy boys, hippies, punks and onwards to those of us who called it 'acieeeeed'. But as my friend Ben said to me the other day, my generation has struck lucky again. "In years to come people will look back and say to us, 'I can't believe you watched every minute of all first four series of Big Brother!'" And these words would be spoken enviously.

Caspar Llewellyn Smith, *The Observer*

Everywhere I have been this summer, I've met people whose professed aim in life is to find a way out of the conceptual crisis created by postmodernism.

Charlotte Raven, *New Statesman*

Everything he has to say about Dylan is original. [Christopher] Ricks is a critic who seems to be talking to you from within the work. He can turn the smallest niche in a poem or a song into a vast cathedral of resonance and implication. On the album *Self Portrait*, for example, there is a song that consists solely of the lines "All the tired horses in the sun/How'm I s'posed to get any ridin' done?/ Hmmm." Ricks devotes four pages to this, bringing in Keats, Tennyson, Marlowe, Shakespeare, Gilbert & Sullivan and Browning before, brilliantly, establishing the theme of sloth that permeates the album.

Bryan Appleyard, *Sunday Times*

A touch of calculated self-parody was once one of Martin Amis's stauncher allies. "Keith finished his fourth Bramley Apple Pie and said, 'Shut it'": this is genius.

Christopher Tayler, *London Review of Books*

There are certain advantages to being my children: they travel and get a sophisticated geopolitical sense of the world.

Sting interviewed on breakfast TV

Some nights it's like pushing an elephant upstairs, but then suddenly that elephant starts to run and it's that fleeting moment that amazes me... it's like a zen experience. You see so many acts who don't even get the elephant to the fuckin' stairs. I think that's why The Who is still valuable.

Roger Daltrey, *The Guardian*

Before a short service at Darlington crematorium on Tuesday of last week, his coffin was placed by the fireplace at the Town Hall and he was toasted by friends, family and former customers.

Darlington & Stockton Times

Disgusting mess floating around pontoons and harbour walls

Dorset Echo

TRURO'S Town Hall in Boscawen Street is to be called the "Town Hall", councillors decided this week.

The West Briton

Walter 56, slightly disabled, seeks sex with men of any age. Must be hairy around Walsall area.

Manzone

Pope sells 23 pubs to ease huge debt

Daily Echo, Bournemouth

5 Live Sports Extra *Digital only*
10.15–12.30pm Rugby World Cup
France v Fifi, live from Brisbane.

Radio Times

SOLUTIONS

Column Solutions

Sir,

I wondered if you might start a new "spotter" column – along the lines of Neophiliacs, Luvvies, etc – for the increasingly prevalent, already clichéd and somehow pretentious use of "Solutions" in company titles and subtitles, and in advertising in general.

For example (all real examples I've seen recently):

Not storage, but Storage Solutions

Not furniture, but Furniture Solutions

Not cardboard boxes, but Packaging Solutions

Not signage, but Sign Solutions

Not a payroll bureau, but Business Solutions

Not a diet, but Slimming Solutions

Not a plumber, but Plumbing Solutions!

This letter has been prompted by my favourite to date: I just had a Sandwich Solution for lunch!

Kind regards,
ANNA C, Via email.

Life solutions

Sir,

I completely agree with your correspondent about the overuse of the word "solutions". One I saw on a lorry recently proudly proclaimed it to be "delivering logistics solutions". In other words – it's a lorry.

> *Kind regards,*
> *VINCENT SWEENEY, Via email.*

Sir,

For some months now, Tesco has catered for its problem eaters by directing them to aisles containing "Chinese Meal Solutions", "Indian Meal Solutions", "Italian Meal Solutions"...

> *MARIAN SMALES, York.*

"Bra Solutions" – *bras*.

"Safe and Efficient Vertical Access Solutions" – *lifts*.

"Sustainable Drainage Solutions" – *drains*.

"BT voice solutions" – *phone lines*.

"Flexible Liquid Transfer Solutions" – *hoses*.

"Lowepro Vision: Carrying Solutions for the Imaging World" – *camera bags*.

"Construction Industry Solutions"
– *builders*.

"The TMK Motorized Impeller, another Air Moving Solution" – *fan*.

"Compass Group... developing and delivering original food and service solutions" – *school dinners*.

"Providing Candidate/Role Synergy Solutions" – *recruitment agency*.

"Smart Christmas Solutions" – *decorations*.

"Smart Gift Solutions" – *presents*.

"Christmas Ornament Storage Solutions cleverly designed so that you no longer have to painstakingly wrap each Christmas ornament in tissue paper in order to protect it" – *cardboard boxes*.

"I wish I could make more movies. The fact that I have some lines on my face, that's it. It's not because I lost my talent or I became deformed" – **Melanie Griffith, who is starring in the Broadway production of Chicago.**

Lincolnshire Echo

CLASS A
Eggs from caged hens living in carefully controlled conditions
Allergy advice: Contains **egg**.

Supermarket carton

28 *The Guardian* Thursday September 18 2003

Grauniad

roast chicken salad — Now with roast chicken

M&S label

AGONY AND ECSTASY SEX WITH DR THOMAS STUTTAFORD AND HANNAH BETTS

The Times

5.15 The Weakest Link; Party Conference Broadcast. By the Labour Party. 5913265
6.05 Get a New Life (R) 245197

Northern Echo

LUVVIES

Gems from the acting profession

"Calling Trevor a director is like calling
Michelangelo a decorator."

> Don Black, Variety Club tribute to Trevor Nunn

"When I let up from the weed and the drinking too,
I cried every day. And I liked that. I like crying.
And now I not only wanna cry and show my crying
to other people, I wanna just split myself down the
middle and open my guts and just throw everything
out!"

> Woody Harrelson, *The Guardian*

"Until very recently I just couldn't wear wool. Eugh.
But then somebody said to me, Jeff, there are some
cashmere garments that would really add to your life.
Don't just block them out. So I gave them a chance
and I've been very much enjoying them ever since."

> Jeff Goldblum, *Sunday Telegraph*

Hello. How are the rehearsals going?
"Intense and inspiring. If acting is a muscle,
Katie Mitchell our director is an Olympic trainer.
Weeping has been heard in the toilets. I save my
tears for the cycle home."

Ben Daniels, Independent On Sunday

Lisa Kudrow told reporters recently that there are
just a few things that really scare her. The *Friends*
star says that while she enjoyed spending the
summer in France with her husband's family, she
hated to shop. "Things are different," she explains.
"We went to the market grocery shopping and
there's no one to bag the groceries, and to me that's
shocking... In some stores you have to bring your
own bag, or buy them."

entertainment.msn.com

24

"I am so lucky, I want to vomit every day. Being able to do exactly what you want is just the most amazing thing in the world."

Drew Barrymore, *Metro*

"We are doing a different play every night, I swear to God. Last night was our 50th show and Patrick [Stewart] and I came off after Act Two and we were shaking. We were trembling with the newness and the freshness. I am going to be heartbroken when it's over."

Lisa Dillon, *The Times*

What have been your most memorable London meals?
"Mezzo with [producer] Stephen Evans. He suggested champagne to cure my hangover. He then asked if I could write a treatment for Lorna Sage's *Bad Blood*. Afterwards I vomited copiously outside Our Price. It was a prelapsarian moment, but now seems quite portentous."

Emily Mortimer, *ES Magazine*

"In Hollywood integrity is the new must-have. Actors, agents and studio heads are branding themselves as conscious consumers by adding their names to waiting lists for a Toyota Prius, booking natural gas-powered limos, catering parties with organic food and photocopying scripts on recycled paper."

Gina Piccolo, *Los Angeles Times*

 **Awarded for services to toadyism and bootlicking**

"At the Saatchi Gallery, it becomes clear that Hirst is neither a joke nor a poseur, but the real thing. In centuries to come, he will be seen as important an artist as Bacon and Freud – perhaps even the great Turner. Give this gallery a chance and go to see the collection several times. If you do, you will come to understand that Charles Saatchi has given us giants."

Bonnie Greer, *Night And Day* magazine

"He [Jeffrey Archer] has phoned most days from prison and I've taken him out for the day whenever I could. He has lots of projects under wraps, but he's coming back to see his friends and family. He wants to get back to chatting, dining out. The public have wall-to-wall affection for him. He's really terrific with anybody he encounters – he only has a little bit of trouble with the upper echelons of society and journalists."

Art dealer Chris Beetles, *Sunday Telegraph Magazine*

"Alastair Campbell's performance in front of the select committee was bullish, forceful, passionate and executed with staggering conviction. If anything was sexed up it was the spin doctor in his crisp white shirt and macho charisma proving among Westminster's hand-wringing, lily-livered apologists there's at least one man prepared to say boo to a goose.

"It's widely alleged Campbell is really the man running the country. Thank God for that."

Sue Carroll, former colleague of
Campbell's, *Daily Mirror*

"Already an icon of beauty and fashion, Zara [Phillips] is imbued with enormous equestrian talent."

Lucinda Green, *Daily Telegraph*

Warballs

"Trinity students have been shocked by a massive rent hike proposed by the college... In a letter to undergraduates the head of the college, the Hon. Michael Beloff QC, cites 'the war in Iraq, concerns about terrorism and now Sars' as contributory reasons for the increases."

Cherwell

Q: My son has earned the rank of Eagle Scout, and I understand the CIA will send him a letter of congratulations upon request?
A: We regret we are unable to process and provide certificates of congratulations to the fine young Americans who have become Eagle Scouts. We have curtailed some activities in order for us to concentrate on the War on Terrorism. Please be assured we will resume the practice when we are able to do so.

From the FAQ section of the CIA website

"A sharp increase in violent assaults and fights has been recorded in Oxfordshire in the past year. But police blamed the increase on new crime-recording methods and the effects of the war in Iraq."

Oxford Times

"A federal judge ruled this week that 9/11 victims and their families can proceed with lawsuits alleging negligence on the part of their fellow victims in the aviation industry and at New York's World Trade Center.

"Such claims may strike some as unjust. But the ruling is legally sound, and the orderly sorting out of responsibilities is a sign, in its way, that terrorists have not undermined American principles and processes, which remain fully functional and characteristically feisty."

Saint Paul Pioneer Press,
Minnesota, 11 September 2003

"A trainee manager at Spearmint Rhino was sacked and threatened with a drugs bust after he reported that lapdancers were breaking the rules by offering sex for cash, a tribunal heard yesterday... Spearmint Rhino insists Mr Singh was made redundant in April because of a drop in customers caused by adverse publicity and the knock-on effects of the 11 September terror outrages of 2001."

Daily Telegraph

"Modernism died on September 11... At a time of mourning people no longer wanted panoramic views across a river out of vast glass windows... Sales of glass and steel furniture plummeted, while sales of burgundy mohair throws rocketed."

Laurence Llewelyn-Bowen, *Observer Food Monthly*

"In her Manhattan lab, [Cindy] Sherman is putting the final touches to an exciting new series, the first to use digital technology. They are large portraits of clowns, all played by Sherman herself... Sherman says she embarked on the clown after 11 September, an event that heralded the end of irony for her."

The Observer

"After the tragedy of the 11 September attacks and the Afghanistan war, Jerszy Seymour decided to design a seat which 'would give the world a great big hug and bring everybody together'. The result was Muffdaddy. Made from machine-washable denim covers with removable polyurethane cushions, Muffdaddy is easy to clean and maintain."

Display at the Design Museum, London

"For some women, handbags are like children. My friend Maggie remembers the exact date she bought her Marc Jacobs. 'It was 25 September 2001. It was post-9/11, and Giuliani was telling everyone to shop. I allowed myself to spend the $750 because I was doing my patriotic duty. It was good for the economy...' A good bag can unite the world... Does she ever use the Marc Jacobs? 'No,' she says, plaintively, 'I've moved on.'"

Ariel Leve, *Sunday Times* Style section

"Who should lead the rebuilding of Iraq? Join our panel and register to win a new convertible!"

internetsurveypanel.com

"September 11th. Some think that dogs don't know about death, or remember our now dead friends. They are wrong. We remember. 'September 11th' by George Hall is available at 11"x14" and 16"x20"."

Ad in *New Yorker* for photo of dog
($375 framed or $275 unframed)

"A firm which struggled to cope after Delia Smith praised its omelette pan has gone bust... A spokesman blamed the problems facing the air industry since the 11 September outrage."

Daily Mirror

From Cambridge to Downing Street? Michael Howard, seated, in the centre, in his student days. Kenneth Clarke is standing, on the right.

The Times

AROUND THE UK NOW

ENGLAND
Sex disease clinics 'cannot cope'
NORTHERN IRELAND
Northern Ireland mourns the Pope
SCOTLAND
Scotland's tribute to late Pope
WALES
Wales mourning death of the Pope

BBC Website, 3 April 2005

New compensation rules for late flights delayed by a year

The Times

NEWS QUIZ
1. a quiz answer; 2. a quiz answer; 3. a quiz answer; 4. a quiz answer a quiz answer a quiz answer; 5. a quiz answer a quiz answer

The Times

D∪MB BRITAIN

Anne Robinson: What was the name of the poet who wrote 'Ode To A Grecian Urn' in 1819?
Contestant: John Gielgud.

The Weakest Link

Anne Robinson: 'Achtung' is a word for warning in which European language?
Contestant: Chinese.

The Weakest Link

Anne Robinson: In what language, spoken in part of the United Kingdom, was the hymn Guide Me O Thou Great Redeemer originally written?
Contestant: Islam.

The Weakest Link

Jodie Marsh: Arrange these two groups of letters to form a word – CHED and PIT.
Team: Chedpit.

Fort Boyard, Challenge TV

Anne Robinson: When a cricket player is said to have scored a century, how many runs has he scored?
Contestant: Two.

The Weakest Link

Anne Robinson: Hadrian's Wall was built to keep out which tribe, the Picts or the Zulus?
Contestant: The Zulus.

The Weakest Link

Anne Robinson: Can you complete the title of the book by Jerome K. Jerome, "Three Men In A..."?
Contestant: Baby.

The Weakest Link

Anne Robinson: Which Roman poet wrote the Aeneid – Virgil or Brains?
Contestant: Brains.

The Weakest Link

Presenter: What happened in Dallas on November 22nd, 1963?
Contestant: I don't know, I wasn't watching it then.

GWR FM, Bristol

Anne Robinson: In ancient mythology, how many labours did Hercules do?
Contestant: One.

The Weakest Link

Anne Robinson: Which country has the largest number of Portuguese speakers in the world?
Contestant: Spain.

The Weakest Link

Ken Bruce: The brothers Derek and Alan Longmuir were members of which famous boy band of the '70s?
Contestant: The Osmonds?
Ken Bruce: Noooo, they tended to be called Osmond, as a rule.

Radio 2

Nick Knowles: Which island was awarded the George Cross during the second World War?
Contestant: France.

Judgemental, BBC1

Anne Robinson: In the 18th century, when Scottish crofters were evicted from their cottages, it was known as the Highland... what?
Contestant: Fling.

The Weakest Link

Anne Robinson: In the 1940s which politician was responsible for the introduction of the Welfare State: William...?
Contestant: The Conqueror.

The Weakest Link

Anne Robinson: The director of the 1956 film The Ten Commandments was Cecil B who?
Contestant: Parkinson.

The Weakest Link

Eamonn Holmes: There are three states of matter: solid, liquid and what?
Contestant: Jelly.

National Lottery Jet Set, BBC1

Anne Robinson: The 19th-century novel by the Russian author Dostoevsky is 'Crime And...' what?
Contestant: Prejudice.

The Weakest Link

Anne Robinson: Kate Hudson is the daughter of which famous American movie actress?
Contestant: Rock.

The Weakest Link

Anne Robinson: Which country lies directly east of South Korea?
Contestant: North Korea.

The Weakest Link

Anne Robinson: What was the relationship between the novelist Evelyn Waugh and the journalist Auberon Waugh?
Contestant: Sister.

The Weakest Link

Anne Robinson: The action of which Shakespeare play takes place between dusk on January 5th and dawn on January 6th?
Contestant: A Midsummer Night's Dream.

The Weakest Link

Eamonn Holmes: Which chapel ceiling did Michelangelo famously paint?
Contestant: The sixteenth chapel.

National Lottery Jet Set, BBC1

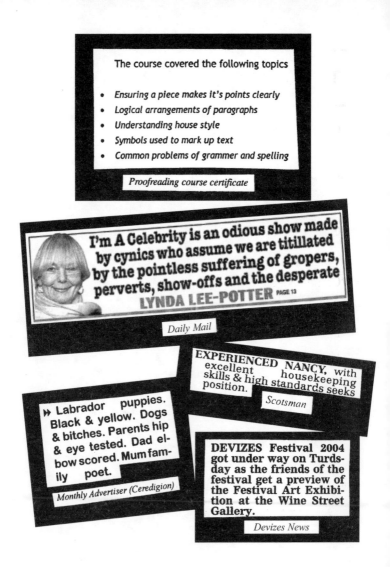

The course covered the following topics

- *Ensuring a piece makes it's points clearly*
- *Logical arrangements of paragraphs*
- *Understanding house style*
- *Symbols used to mark up text*
- *Common problems of grammer and spelling*

Proofreading course certificate

I'm A Celebrity is an odious show made by cynics who assume we are titillated by the pointless suffering of gropers, perverts, show-offs and the desperate
LYNDA LEE-POTTER PAGE 13

Daily Mail

EXPERIENCED NANCY, with excellent housekeeping skills & high standards seeks position.

Scotsman

▶ Labrador puppies. Black & yellow. Dogs & bitches. Parents hip & eye tested. Dad elbow scored. Mum family poet.

Monthly Advertiser (Ceredigion)

DEVIZES Festival 2004 got under way on Turds-day as the friends of the festival get a preview of the Festival Art Exhibition at the Wine Street Gallery.

Devizes News

THE NEOPHILIACS

"Cheese is the new chocolate."

Living South magazine

"Noodles are the new pizza."

The Grocer magazine

"Chocolate is the new olive oil."

New York Times

"Could chocolate be the new cough medicine?"

BBC News online

"Fish is the new steak."

Jill Dupleix, *The Times*

"Mangoes are definitely the new kiwi fruit."

Caterer and Licensee

"Water is the new tea."

The Guardian

"Duck is the new chicken."

The Nation's Favourite Food, BBC2

"Ice cream is the new Atkins."

BBC News online

"Are transfatty acids the new tobacco?"
You And Yours, Radio 4

"Saturday is the new Sunday."
Financial Times

"Is Monday the new Friday?"
New York Times

"Thursday is now the new Friday."
Suzi Godson, *Independent On Sunday*

"Why Sunday is the new Saturday night."
Sydney Morning Herald

"Four in the morning is the new teatime."
ES magazine

"September is the new January."
The Guardian

"Why September is the new August."
Western Mail

"January is the new August."
Sunday Times

"Hallowe'en is the new Christmas."
The Guardian

"Barcelona is the new Paris."

Daily Telegraph

"Bath is the new Paris."

Bath Chronicle

"Skye is the new Azores."

Financial Times

"Could Dubrovnik be the new St. Tropez?"

The Times

"Ibiza – the new Saint Tropez."

Lisa Armstrong, *The Times*

"Dubrovnik, apparently, is the new Guildford."

Rod Liddle, *Sunday Times*

"Croatia emerges as the new Tuscany."

Daily Telegraph

"Perhaps south-east England is the new Tuscany."

Rose Shepherd, *The Times*

"Bulgaria is the new Benidorm."

The Independent

"Bratislava – the new Manhattan?"

Guardian Unlimited

"Mesopotamia is the new Egypt."

Archaeologist Eleanor Robson, *Oxford Today*

Petersfield £650,000

A charming Grade II listed period house dating back we understand to the time of the dissolution of the monasteries, standing in lovely gardens of about 0.25 acres and with a large stone barn suitable for a variety of uses.

Master bedroom and dressing room, 3 further bedrooms, bathroom, 2 cloakroom, sitting room, dining room, kitchen. large stone barn with extensive internal space, lovely walled gardens of about 0.25 acres, garage, parking.

Petersfield Herald

Name change

DYER'S Court in Beechwood Avenue, Woodley, is to be known as The Chestnuts – after town councillors decided it was not a very appropriate name for an old people's home.

Reading Chronicle

Pseuds
Corner

I've taken to long-distance walking as a means of dissolving the mechanised matrix which compresses the space-time continuum, and decouples humans from physical geography.

Will Self, *Independent Magazine*

Whenever I go back to Selfridges these days I feel like Le Grand Meaulnes, questing in vain for his vanished domain.

James Delingpole 'on his constant search for the perfect pair of denims', *The Times*

Huso's sculptures are an observation on the female menstrual cycle and are intended to raise the eyebrows of both men and women bemused by this age-old taboo... Using recycled materials such as bicycles, handbags and telephones, in combination with her preferred medium of organic cotton tampons and natural sanitary pads, Huso has created a unique and striking collection of what she terms 'T.art' work for this debut solo exhibition.

Right On – a new collection of conceptual sculptures by Lyn Huso, Coningsbury Gallery, London

I experimented with it [television] for a year but found it intrusive, especially the BBC news presentation. The signature tune was E major. Such a special key, reserved for works like Bruckner's Seventh Symphony and Beethoven's Opus 109 Sonata.

Peter Maxwell Davies, *The Guardian*

Fairy cakes. The *fons et origo* of my cupcake passion.

Nigella Lawson, *Sainsbury's Magazine*

I used to carry a copy of *Ulysses* with me everywhere just in case I was knocked down by a bus. It seemed more important than having clean underwear.

Craig Raine, *The Guardian*

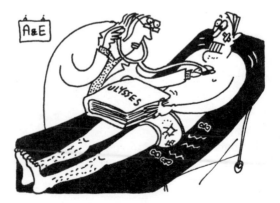

A class warrior, dandy and intellectual, [Mark E] Smith is one of nature's aristocrats. Born and raised in Salford, he is now resident in Prestwich, North Manchester. His performances with The Fall – delivering the elaborate code of his lyrics in plosive, spoken bursts from the corner of his mouth, across rigid, relentless repetitions of rock chords – can seem virtually shamanic. He is Beuysian in this respect.

Michael Bracewell, *Guardian Weekend*

I regularly buy only the *Telegraph*, getting my other information from *Le Monde* and the *Wall Street Journal* (much improved since being reinforced in its European edition by the *Washington Post*). I often buy the *Corriere della Sera* and *La Vanguardia*, of Barcelona, and also like to pick and choose among the other dailies now easily available in London, such as the *Manila Times* and the *Buenos Aires Herald.*

Paul Johnson, *The Spectator*

I have long been under the impression that fellatio fell into desuetude with the decline of the Roman Empire and the Gothic desolation of the communal bath, to return to fashion in France in the age of Toulouse-Lautrec, at the height of the perfume trade and the new etiquette for consuming asparagus.

Brian Sewell, *Evening Standard*

They're going to harden it up. It's not going to be: "My sister is sleeping with my father". It's going to be: "My sister is sleeping with my father, but they're both interested in the Middle East".

Nicky Campbell on his new TV chat show, *The Observer*

After a long day spent looking at fabrics and computer screens, I don't want to just watch television or go to the cinema; I want to interact with other people. I went to the Oscars ceremony recently just so that I could catch up on what was happening in the movies.

Nicky Haslam, *Harpers & Queen*

On her wrist she [Tracey Emin] wears black sea pearls... and two gold bangles. She bought these in Istanbul to replace two bangles that Matt, her ex-boyfriend, had given her, after they broke up. Because, as she explains to me, complete with an enthusiastic mime, "It wouldn't be right to be giving someone a handjob wearing bangles another man had given you." In her own way, Emin is a true romantic.

Jess Cartner-Morley, *The Guardian*

Music is being detached from the unsynthesised manifold.

Germaine Greer on John Cage's 4 minutes 33 seconds of silence, broadcast by Radio 3, *Late Review*

Jesus beats me hands down. His life was an awesome study in self-destruction. It has been valuable for us to deceive ourselves about the depth of his destructiveness. Clearly, as a great religious stylist, he knew that, without his crucifixion, he would be no one.

Sebastian Horsley, New Statesman

Imagine footballers in the form of water (and why not? it's the one element that flows through our daily lives) and what do you see? Kenny Dalglish as a river, perhaps, a majestic, teeming river, like the Rhine, sweeping past the Lorelei; Eric Cantona as a lake, sparkling like a million diamonds when the sun dances upon the waves but also reflecting the darker moods of a troubled sky. Denis Law as a waterfall, Jimmy Greaves a geyser... Thierry Henry is an ocean.

Michael Henderson, Evening Standard

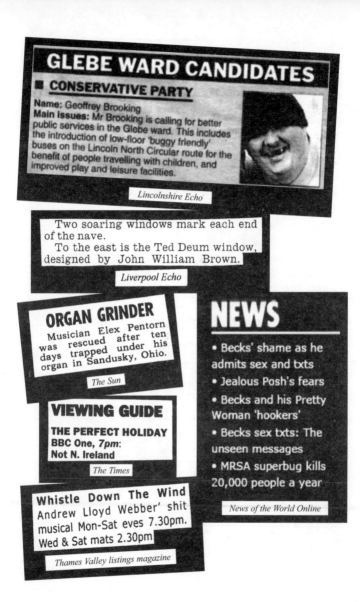

GLEBE WARD CANDIDATES

■ CONSERVATIVE PARTY

Name: Geoffrey Brooking
Main issues: Mr Brooking is calling for better public services in the Glebe ward. This includes the introduction of low-floor 'buggy friendly' buses on the Lincoln North Circular route for the benefit of people travelling with children, and improved play and leisure facilities.

Lincolnshire Echo

Two soaring windows mark each end of the nave.
To the east is the Ted Deum window, designed by John William Brown.

Liverpool Echo

ORGAN GRINDER
Musician Elex Pentorn was rescued after ten days trapped under his organ in Sandusky, Ohio.

The Sun

VIEWING GUIDE
THE PERFECT HOLIDAY
BBC One, *7pm*:
Not N. Ireland

The Times

Whistle Down The Wind
Andrew Lloyd Webber' shit musical Mon-Sat eves 7.30pm. Wed & Sat mats 2.30pm

Thames Valley listings magazine

NEWS

- Becks' shame as he admits sex and txts
- Jealous Posh's fears
- Becks and his Pretty Woman 'hookers'
- Becks sex txts: The unseen messages
- MRSA superbug kills 20,000 people a year

News of the World Online

DUMB BRITAIN

Graeme Garden: The Ashmolean in Oxford was England's first what?
Contestant: Indian restaurant.

Beat The Nation, C4

Anne Robinson: William Burroughs's novel, first published in 1959, was 'The Naked...' what?
Contestant: Chef.

The Weakest Link

Darren Lee: Shiraz, Chardonnay and Chablis are all names of what?
Contestant: Footballers' wives.

Chiltern FM

Anne Robinson: Ginger Rogers and Fred Astaire first appeared together in the film 'Flying Down To...' where?
Contestant: Halifax.

The Weakest Link

Gaby Logan: Who is considered to be the first British Prime Minister?
Contestant: Harold Wilson.
Brokers: Cromwell? Churchill? Margaret Thatcher?

The Vault

Stewart White: Who had a worldwide hit with the song 'What A Wonderful World'?

Contestant: I don't know.

White: Okay, I'll give you a couple of clues. What do you call the part of your body between your hand and your elbow?

Contestant: The arm.

White: Correct! And if you aren't weak, you are...?

Contestant: Strong.

White: Correct. And a final clue: what was Lord Mountbatten's first name?

Contestant: Louis.

White: Well there we are then. So who did have a worldwide hit with the song 'What A Wonderful World'?

Contestant: Frank Sinatra?

BBC Radio Norfolk

Presenter: Which Scotsman discovered penicillin in 1928?

Contestant: Alexander Penicillin.

TalkSport

Anne Robinson: What is the only even prime number?

Contestant: Nine.

The Weakest Link

Eamonn Holmes: What does the French phrase "Je t'aime" mean?

Contestant: Goodbye.

National Lottery Jet Set, BBC1

Anne Robinson: In what year did the First World War end?
Contestant: 1948.

The Weakest Link

Den Siergertsz: An isosceles triangle has how many sides of equal length? It's not three or four. How many?
Contestant: Hang on, I'm just working it out. *(Pause.)* Eight.

BBC Radio Stoke

Anne Robinson: Which B completes the title of this book written by Lord Baden-Powell: "Scouting For..."?
Contestant: Business.

The Weakest Link

God Bless America: With God On Our Side
7.20pm Saturday 30th October, Channel 4

What makes George W Bush tick? Providing a definitive examination of the rise of the religious right in the US and Bush's own religious re-birth, which took him from heavy drinking and a failing business to set him on the path to the White House.

The Human Chimp
8.00pm Sunday 31st October, five

TV Highlights, virgin.net

"She's in a lovely costume. It's a big green dress, and you can clearly see her in the court scene. As the actors walk forward, you can see her behind."

Scarborough Evening News

Many have large markets outside the Islamic world – among them Koc Holding, a Turkish conglomerate whose subsidiaries include Arcelik, which sells household appliances across Europe.

Economist on line

This new organization will enable Johnson & Johnson to better address the needs of patients around the world who require treatment for heart failure and sudden cardiac death.

Johnson & Johnson Press Release

Yaris owner's manual

'Darcy's Dilemma'
Sunday, December 14th
A special day in Jane Austen's Bath.

Country Neighbour (Basildon)

"May I say to the House that it is good to see the Prime Minister here on top form, fighting inequality as usual?"

Joan Walley MP

"Miss Jowell is convinced that Mr Blair has no plans to give up. She says the party forgot how much it owed him when it almost failed to support him in the tuition fee debate. 'I would jump in front of a bus to save him,' she says."

Daily Telegraph

"Gordon Brown is a warm and caring man and he possesses that rare quality – lacking in so many of his colleagues – he listens. That's why Wednesday's budget saw him help pensioners and pour billions into schools and the NHS."

Fiona Phillips, *Daily Mirror*

"Since reading this book, I have been unable to get Jane Fonda out of my head. She is a remarkable woman, and My Life So Far, which is an unusually worthwhile autobiography, bears the firm imprint of her complex, febrile and essentially noble character."

Laura Thompson, *Daily Telegraph*

"Think dark, think brooding, think masterful and in control. Watching Gordon Brown delivering his annual budget is one of the highlights of my TV year. All those clever sums – whatever he produced from his box, there is always the tantalising possibility that this man might have a clever formula between the sheets."

Sharon Hendry, "TV's Sexiest Scenes", *The Sun*

"The best holiday read this summer is unfortunately published in September. Boris Johnson's novel *Seventy-Two Virgins* is what I had previously considered oxymoronic, a comic thriller. A bicycling MP who fears that he is about to be exposed by the newspapers for a sexual scandal gets caught up in an al-Qa'eda plot against an American president. It is an effortlessly brilliant page-turner. Boris is a jack of all trades and a master of them."

Sarah Sands, *Daily Telegraph*

"Erin [O'Connor], please don't despair. You are elegant, endearing, intelligent, witty, warm, gracious, gentle, gorgeous, smart, successful, down-to-earth and fashion fabulous. God, we don't even know you, but we love you!"

Sunday Times Style magazine

"It is too often forgotten that Cherie Blair is one of the most brilliant women of her generation. If she had never met Tony Blair she would now be a High Court judge or maybe a Cabinet minister."

Peter Oborne, *Evening Standard*

"Of all the Old Etonians in the House of Commons today, only Oliver Letwin carries any authority, and what makes him so distinctive, so head and shoulders above his contemporaries, so effortlessly superior, is not what he learned at school but what he learned from his beautiful American academic mother, Shirley Letwin, rightly famous as the author of that most enthusiastic and eloquent celebration of the English gentleman, her classic work *The Gentleman in Trollope: Individuality and Moral Conduct* (1982)."

Peregrine Worsthorne,
In Defence of Aristocracy (2004)

"If you want to know what today's teenagers are thinking, you're better off reading *The Spectator* than *The Face*."

Toby Young, *Daily Telegraph*

SOLUTIONS

"Picture Hanging Solutions" – *packet of hooks.*

"Vehicle Remarketing Solutions" – *second-hand cars.*

"Entry Control Solutions" – *turnstiles.*

"Total document solutions" – *paper and ink for computer printers.*

"Total Move Solutions" – *estate agents.*

"Total domestic ventilation solutions" – *windows.*

"Aperture Solutions" – *windows.*

"Progressive Fenestration Solutions" – *windows.*

"SleepingSolutions.co.uk" – *beds.*

"Human-powered solutions" – *bicycles.*

"Expense claim solutions" – *taxi receipts.*

"Bisley: Storage solutions in steel" – *filing cabinets.*

"Raytheon: Mission Solutions for the Warfighter" – *weapons*.

"Isle of Man Post: Integrated Mailing Solutions" – *post*.

"Sericol – more than ink: Solutions" – *ink*.

"Organic magnify-your-member solution" – *penis enlargement spam email*.

"Macfarlane Group: passionate about providing total packaging solutions" – *cardboard boxes, pots, bottles and bags*.

"Concord: a family of turnkey, automated, scaleable, software-based performance analysis and reporting solutions" – *timesheets*.

"IPSO Stainless Laundry Solutions" – *washing machines*.

"Jonathan Fry & Co. Bespoke Wealth Preservation Solutions" – *financial advisers*.

"Swisher: The Total Washroom Solution" – *toilet cleaners*.

"Fastsigns: digital sign solutions, signage and other signs solutions" – *signs*.

THE mystery fan behind the takeover bid for Port Vale today said he will pull out of the deal if his identity is revealed.

It is understood Stone-based businessman Peter Jackson wants to remain anonymous until the contract is signed and sealed.

Staffordshire Sentinel

The Home Secretary took his lover and her two-year-old son William to the upmarket resort of St Stephano at the end of May.

Weeks later, Mr Quinn was proudly telling friends that his wife was expecting their second child and that it was a 'miracle' baby, conceived without the help of infertility treatment. Now he has had to concede the baby is almost certainly Mr Blunkett.

Daily Mail

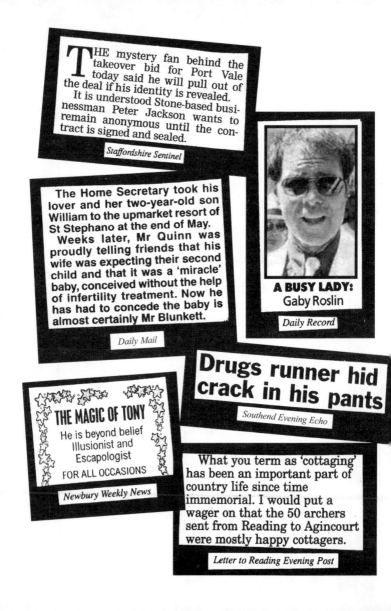

A BUSY LADY:
Gaby Roslin

Daily Record

Drugs runner hid crack in his pants

Southend Evening Echo

THE MAGIC OF TONY
He is beyond belief
Illusionist and
Escapologist
FOR ALL OCCASIONS

Newbury Weekly News

What you term as 'cottaging' has been an important part of country life since time immemorial. I would put a wager on that the 50 archers sent from Reading to Agincourt were mostly happy cottagers.

Letter to Reading Evening Post

LUVVIES

"I don't know how else to put it," the recently-knighted Kingsley told the *New York Daily News*. "Before, I was acting more for myself. Now I'm doing it for my country because my country has asked me to."

Sir Ben Kingsley

"I would *love* to get everybody in the world thinking the same thing just for one second. I bet you something mental would happen. Even if we all just thought 'cup of tea'."

James McAvoy, *Scotland On Sunday*

The singer [Norah Jones] doesn't watch television that often, she said, and doesn't even have cable. Instead, she prefers to read.

"I've always loved to read, but sometimes I go for a year without reading a book because I forget to, or I don't have a book that I can get into easily," she said.

AP Entertainment News

"We're like very delicate china right now," said star Jennifer Aniston, who plays Rachel in the show. "And we're going to smash into a million pieces," added Lisa Kudrow, who plays Phoebe in the show. "It's a deeper loss than I was expecting."

BBC Online

"We were doing this scene in the morgue, and I'm lying on the table, my eyes closed, and the energy that was coming off Sean [Penn] was so powerful I started to cry. And Clint Eastwood says, 'Cut, Emmy, that was great, but you can't cry. You're dead.'"

Emmy Rossum, *Vanity Fair*

"Earlier this year I had my hair feng-shuied."

Jerry Hall, *Sunday Times*

"The phrase 'seen and heard' has always stayed with me, as an explanation for who I am, and what I do with who I am. When I received the letter from Tony Blair to say I was receiving a knighthood, it meant the country had said 'We have seen you and we have heard you.' I found it beautiful."

Sir Ben Kingsley, *Hotdog magazine*

"My physical and emotional selves were a total mess, but Doctor Theatre is very potent – especially if you're rehearsing with great performers."

Sir Peter Hall, *Sunday Times*

"I don't want to be the voice of a generation, yet I have felt that thrust upon me."

Chloe Sevigny, *Sunday Times Magazine*

"Film-making is like the First World War," he says, swilling back the last of his tea, and uncrossing his long legs. "It just grinds you down. All you can do is focus simply on surviving it."

John Cleese, *The Independent*

"I didn't know much about Pinter," she pronounces matter-of-factly. "I haven't seen many of his productions before. I only had this vague idea of black polo necks and Gitanes – incredibly intellectual. But actually, when I read the play my reaction to it was, 'God, this man must be good in bed.'"

Helen McCrory, *Evening Standard*

Lenny Henry: much-loved comic cuddle-bunny

Financial Times

LADY, reasonable looks, medium build, 65, likes short walks, outings, the occasional drunk.

Westmorland Gazette

LOVING female 49, slim/medium build, many interests, seeks that special, kind, caring, honest gut, to share life with.

Hull Daily Mail

Councillor Coleman has argued that the council's case against lap dancing was strengthened by the publication of a report, which it commissioned, which argued that most men go to the cubs for sexual services.

Scottish Licensed Trade

THE NEOPHILIACS

"50 is the new 40; 60 is the new 50."

Patricia Hewitt, *Daily Telegraph*

"We used to say that 50 was the new 40, but now I wonder if it's not the new 32 and a half."

Emma Soames, *Evening Standard*

"52 is the new 30."

Jeremy Vine, Radio 2

"40 is the new 21."

John Scott, *This Morning*, ITV

"Why 90 is the new 70."

Katharine Whitehorn, *The Guardian*

"8 is the new 15."

The Times fashion supplement

"Gambling. It's the new yoga."

Sunday Times Style section

"Face yoga – it's the new Botox."

Evening Standard

"Botox is the new heroin."

Sunday Times Style section

"Opera could well be the new cocaine."

Irish Times

"Painting is the new taxidermy."

Daily Telegraph

"Spelling is the new punctuation."

John Humphrys, *The Times*

"Scrap metal is the new irony."

Daily Telegraph motoring section

"Ladders are the new sugar."

Jo Whiley, Radio 1

"Irrelevance: the new relevance."

Grist magazine

"Six months is the new two years."

Richard Madeley, Channel 4

"Celebrity is the new glue."

Financial Times

"Camping is the new taramasalata."

The Independent

"Cartoonishness is the new verisimilitude."

James Wood, *London Review of Books*

"Checking your inbox is the new going out. "

Guardian

"To see mycoplasma genitalium as the new chlamydia is tempting."

The Lancet

"In Honduras today, clothes are the new bananas."

Sean Langan, *Travels With a Gringo*, Channel 4

"At the risk of going into *Private Eye*, I think white pepper is the new black pepper."

Stephen Fry, *Sainsbury's magazine*

Lesbian model wins sex pest case against boss

PICTURE: EMILY BARBER/ 139928-34

JOKE: Prince Andrew

Leicester Mercury

George Foxwell, her lawyer, said: "The applicant's case is that it was implied that if she slept with Miss Hough it would be good for her career. This is a classic case of sexual harassment, someone who is looking for an advantage by using their power and tempting the person with a carrot."

Daily Telegraph

In a grilling by the public on Sky News, the Prime Minister said he was recruiting overseas dentists to fill the gaps.

The Times

"So I tied up his hands and feet and got a kitchen knife to chop off his organ and bring an end to his lust once and for all."

The man, who has not been named, was taken to a local hospital where his penis was re-attacked by doctors.

Sky News web page

Warballs

"The capture of Saddam Hussein could help to make the current holiday sales season the strongest in years for restaurants, a leading industry economist said yesterday."

restaurantbiz.com

"Yoko [Ono] admits that she herself has changed. It came in part after the events of 11 September, when she was in Manhattan. The shock served to arrest her artistic snobbery. Soon after the attacks, she went to an art show and saw how someone had painted a clown on velvet. There was a time when she would have laughed at it. Not any more."

The Independent

"Here's a fact that escaped the 9/11 commission: on the afternoon of the attacks, 42 women called the New York Yves Saint Laurent store to order the label's peasant blouse, that fall's must-have fashion item. What that says about our culture's needs and wants is probably too chilling to contemplate – so don't; just continue to feast your eyes as you turn the pages of *Tom Ford*, a luscious coffee table book out from Rizzoli this month."

Vanity Fair

"Wonderland Sydney, the eastern Creek amusement park that has attracted millions of thrill-seekers for 19 years, will close its gates for the final time in April. Management says 11 September, the Bali bombings, the collapse of insurance giant HIH, the Sars virus and now the Asian bird flu 'have simply taken their toll'."

Sydney Morning Herald

"Britain's first licensed nude strip club, the Raymond Revue Bar, today collapsed into administration after nearly half a century of trading... 9/11, the economic downturn, Sars and avian flu have conspired to decimate takings."

Evening Standard

"A British government scientist who has been to Iraq and worked in the field of chemical and biological warfare was invited to talk to the ladies of Bosham WI to make sure they know exactly what to do in the event of a terrorist strike."

Chichester Observer

"If there is a serious terrorist occurrence in London, clearly the consumer market is just going to die. To be seen next to gruesome editorial is very detrimental to a brand."

Nick Walker of Walker Media, quoted in *Media Week*

"A Texas jury on Monday found a British streaker guilty of criminal trespassing for racing onto the field during the Super Bowl in February with only a thong and a smile... Prosecutor Kristin Gurney argued that Roberts's antics could not be tolerated in post-11 September America. 'As light-hearted about this as I'd like to be, we don't live in a society any more where we can excuse this kind of behaviour,' she told the jury."

Reuters

"But in the aftermath of 9/11, Higham says, coolness has simply lost its lustre. 'If global terrorism means each of us could die tomorrow,' he asks, 'why bother leaving the right book out on the coffee table or having the right haircut?'"

The Times

"A Winnipeg body piercer plans to stick 3,000 surgical needles into his body to commemorate the people who died in the terrorist attacks of Sept 11, 2001. Four people will start sticking the needles in Brent Moffatt, 36, at the moment the first jetliner hit the World Trade Centre's north tower."

Montreal Gazette

"Yesterday L'Oréal reported a 10 percent rise in pre-tax profits to €1.87 bn on sales down 1.8 percent at €14 bn, despite having to cope with some of the worst currency fluctuations in the group's history, the impact of war in Iraq and the outbreak of Sars. 'You can't use lipstick wearing a face mask,' Mr Owen-Jones said."

The Guardian

"Number brands are immediately understood around the world, adds David Haigh, MD of Brand Finance. 7-Up is a great example and 7-Eleven is 'a brilliant number brand: it just shouts convenience,' says Haigh. But perhaps the most potent number brand of all is 9-11. In three years it has become one of the world's most famous brands, associated with the vivid image of New York's burning Twin Towers. Davidson believes the use of number brands has grown since – and possibly as a consequence of – 9/11."

Financial Director magazine

DUMB BRITAIN

Steve Wright: What type of banana is most often used in Caribbean cooking?
Contestant: A yellow one.

Radio 2

Gaby Logan: What is the county town of Kent?
Contestant: Don't know.
Brokers: Kentish Town?

The Vault

Anne Robinson: What name is given to the field of medicine that concerns the health of women?
Contestant: Womenology.

The Weakest Link

Eamonn Holmes: What year is the title of a famous novel by George Orwell?
Contestant: 1949.

National Lottery Jet Set, BBC1

Phil Tufnell: How many Olympic Games have been held?
Contestant: Six!
Phil: Higher!
Contestant: Five!

Simply The Best, ITV

Anne Robinson: The Hallelujah Chorus occurs in which oratorio by Handel?
Contestant: The Sound Of Music.

The Weakest Link

Anne Robinson: What is the more common name given to the government department 'Military Intelligence Six'?
Celebrity hairdresser: MI5.

The Weakest Link

Anne Robinson: Which Tory MP twice stood unsuccessfully for the leadership of the Conservative Party, against William Hague and Iain Duncan Smith?
Contestant *(after much thought)*: Ken Livingstone.

The Weakest Link

Nick Girdler: I'm looking for an island in the Atlantic Ocean whose name includes the letter 'e'.
Contestant: Ghana.
Girdler: No, listen. It's an *island* in the *Atlantic.*
Contestant: New Zealand.

BBC Radio Solent

Jonathon Cowap: If someone is described as hirsute, what are they?
Contestant: Erm.
Cowap: Here's a clue. Most men are, and most women would like us to think they are not.
Contestant (*after long pause*)**:** Is it gay, Jonathon?

BBC Radio York

Anne Robinson: A pain in the muscles or bones of the lower legs, often suffered by sportsmen is known as Shin....?
Contestant: ...dler's List.

The Weakest Link

Steve Wright: What do you call a dead person who has been canonised?
Contestant: A bishop.

Radio 2

Anne Robinson: Mount Everest is in the autonomous Chinese region of Tibet and which other country?
Contestant: Nicaragua.

The Weakest Link

Jamie Theakston: Which 19th-century author wrote Lady Windermere's Fan?
Contestant *(having had several minutes to think about it and discuss it with other contestants)***:** Ben Elton.

Beg, Borrow Or Steal, BBC2

Jamie Theakston: Which university is named after the designer of the Great Western Railway?
Contestant *(following discussion with other contestants)***:** Cambridge.
Theakston: Do you know where Cambridge University is?
Contestant: No. Geography isn't my strongest subject.
Theakston: Well... the clue's in the name.
Contestant: Leicester?

Beg, Borrow Or Steal, BBC2

Ian Wright: What type of creature is a praying mantis?
Contestant: A fish.
Wright: Are you sure you want to say fish?
Contestant *(confidently)***:** Yes, a fish.

National Lottery, BBC1

Steve Wright: What type of headgear is also the name of a film starring Fred Astaire and Ginger Rogers?
Contestant: Bobble hat.

Radio 2

Anne Robinson: In which city is the Scottish Parliament situated?
Former member of Boyzone: London.

The Weakest Link

Ian Wright: Iago and Desdemona are characters in which Shakespeare play?
Contestant: I did English literature at university. *(Pause.)* Hamlet?

National Lottery, BBC1

Anne Robinson: After Guernsey, Jersey and Alderney, what is the next largest of the Channel Islands?
Jodie Marsh: Er... is England a Channel Island?

The Weakest Link

Melanie 'Mel' Sykes: In 2002 the Queen celebrated her Golden Jubilee. In which year did she come to the throne?
Contestant: 1958.
Sykes: No, it was 1952. I wouldn't have got that.
Contestant: No it was far too hard.

Today With Des & Mel, ITV

Anne Robinson: Which humorous poet is famous for such poems as 'Oh! I Wish I'd Looked After Me Teeth' and 'They Should Have Asked My Husband'?
Contestant: Tennyson.

The Weakest Link

Anne Robinson: The title 'Countess' is given to the wife of which rank of the British nobility?
Contestant: Queen.

The Weakest Link

James O'Brien: How many kings of England have been called Henry?
Contestant: Er, well I know there was a Henry the eighth... Er... er... three?

LBC 97.3

Anne Robinson: Single combat is a fight between how many people?
Contestant: One person.

The Weakest Link

Anne Robinson: What 'h' is a common variety of bean used to make baked beans?
Contestant: Heinz.

The Weakest Link

Les Dennis: Name something people believe in but cannot see.
Contestant: Hitler.

Family Fortunes, Challenge TV

Anne Robinson: King Priam was associated with which besieged city?
Contestant: Newcastle.

The Weakest Link

Wright: What is the name of the mountain that overlooks Rio de Janeiro?
Contestant: Er, can I have a clue?
Wright: It's a cute name.
Contestant: Claire?

Steve Wright's Big Quiz, Radio 2

Presenter: Which literary hunchback lived in Notre Dame and fell in love with Esmerelda?
Contestant 1: Nostradamus.
Presenter: No that's not right. I'll have to pass it over.
Contestant 2: Oh, er, it rings a bell... but no, can't think of it.

Brainteaser

Auch ein Grund für die Erhöhung der Hundesteuer in Feldkirchen: Die zunehmenden Verunreinigungen im Gemeindegebiet.
Foto: HALLO-Archiv

Hallo, Munich

Public 'mast' debate
Church plans under attack

Holme Valley Express

Mr A.D. Egan and Miss C.J. Bacon
The engagement is announced between Andrew, son of Mr and Mrs Malcolm Egan, of Guiseley, West Yorkshire, and Caroline, daughter of Mr and Mrs Rodger Bacon, of Kirribilli, New South Wales, Australia.

Daily Telegraph

Pseuds
Corner

It was while removing a particularly adhesive smear of Camembert from the two fluttering birds on a willow-pattern plate that I first understood Beethoven's Grosse Fuge.

Roger Scruton, *The Times*

In the evenings, my companion and I love to pop open a bottle of the local plonk and translate poetry in and out of whichever classical language we currently favour, so I imagine we'll find room in the suitcase for Michael Sokoloff's *Dictionary of Jewish Palestinian Aramaic of the Byzantine Period* (Johns Hopkins University Press).

Hari Kunzru's holiday reading, *The Guardian*

For 'Rubbish Bag in Wanking Corner' (1999) Schneider himself crouched in the bag of the title for seven hours, all-seeing but invisible, and nobody ever knew he was there. 'Die Familie Schneider', his new show in London, features living, breathing, wanking people and represents a startling, and hugely risky, change of direction.

Gordon Burn, *The Guardian*

Among the great novelists perhaps only Balzac
had the range and power to deal properly with the
tragedy which has engulfed my friend and colleague
Kimberly Quinn of *The Spectator* and the Home
Secretary David Blunkett.

Peter Oborne, *Evening Standard*

I haven't got round to changing the battery in my
alarm clock, so I get my assistant to give me a
wake-up call about 10 a.m. instead. I'll then go
downstairs, put on some coffee – always organic,
always decaffeinated – and feed Helix, my dog.
I named him after the chromosome structure that
makes up DNA.

A life in the day of Michael Stipe,
Sunday Times Magazine

The koi were making the usual commotion about their food. I was sitting on an upturned bucket, idly watching them, when I became aware of someone gently walking on my hand, a tiny someone as crisp and fine as if she had been newly blown out of glass... She was a miniature Biedermeier bibelot, in all less than half an inch long. Failing to recognise her would be like failing to recognise Coco Chanel.

Germaine Greer encounters a hoverfly,
Weekend Telegraph

10.15 Late Junction
Fiona Talkington revisits last year's I Trawl The Megahertz by former Prefab Sprout Paddy McAloon. Plus Ingbrigt Haker Flaten's improvisation for double bass on Gershwin's I Loves You, Porgy, and Helge Sten, also known as Deathprod, with his Imaginary Songs From Tristan da Cunha.

Radio 3 schedules

Where did the inspiration for the song 'Crazy Horses' come from?
It was Alan, Wayne and Merrill who wrote 'Crazy Horses'. Wayne and Merrill were in the studio and Wayne had started the main riff for the song. Then Alan came in and brought a cohesive concept about pollution: the horses being horsepower. Then Merrill added the 'crazy' before the horses. It's a very serious song.

Donny Osmond, *The Independent*

Dave Watson in his playing days

Leicester v Plymouth Argyle programme

Outdoor Bowels for the Disabled
Wednesdays, 4pm – 6pm
John Innes Park, Mostyn Road,
Merton Park.

My Merton

"I haven't come here to sit on my backside," said Butt. "I don't think my best days are behind me, I've come here to win more trophies."

Grauniad

Of course one could argue that the Ring Cycle is inherently phallocentric, but having established a potent back-lit image of Kathleen Broderick's feline Brunnhilde in profile, Lloyd blows the final duet by turning Brunnhilde's embrace with Siegfried into a Rorschach blob of such bluntly priapic tumescence as to be far funnier than any amount of witty fire-extinguishers.

Anna Picard, *Independent On Sunday*

John Keats, the Romantic poet, concluded "Ode on a Grecian Urn" with the thought: "Beauty is truth, truth beauty – that is all/Ye know on earth and need to know."

Had Keats been in Los Angeles this week, he could have predicted the winner of the coming video game console battle between Sony's third PlayStation and Microsoft's second Xbox.

John Gapper, *Financial Times*

I have no quarrel with Einstein.

Simon Jenkins, *The Times*

He [Lucian Freud] justifies the existence of paint, as far as I'm concerned.

Sir Peter Hall, *Independent On Sunday*

Writing here last year... I warned of deeper divisions along racial, geographical and gender lines and foresaw the triumph of low-carb diets.

'Trendspotter' Marian Salzman, *Sunday Times*

...now, to make my tea, I need two good-sized mugs. I boil the kettle. The hot water goes into one mug first, stays for a few seconds so the mug is heated, then goes into the second mug. The tea bag goes into the first, hot, mug, boiling water is poured in, to within a couple of millimetres of the top, and the two mugs, one containing brewing tea, and the other containing hot water, are left to stand. After about five minutes, the mug of brewed tea is placed in the sink, where some new hot water (freshly re-boiled) from the kettle, is sloshed into it, so it overflows by about half a mug. This is to stop the well-brewed tea being too strong. The full-to-overflowing mug is now tilted a little bit, so it spills out enough tea to allow room for some milk.

Remember the second mug, full of the hot (now not so hot, but still quite hot) water that was used to warm the first mug? That is now emptied. The tea bag is fished out from the first 'brewing' mug and placed in the bottom of the empty 'warm' mug, where a small splash of warm milk is poured over it. The effect of the hot tea bag, and still-warm milk, is to take the chill off the milk... *[continues for quite some while]*

> Hugh Fearnley-Whittingstall makes a cup of tea,
> *Observer Food Magazine*

Most people don't do something seminal. I've done it twice: with my tent and my bed. Picasso did it with Cubism.

> Tracey Emin, *Desert Island Discs*, Radio 4

I thought first of the next pope. I've often noticed how bishops, of all Christian denominations, have never read Adam Smith, but know intuitively that they disagree with him. My first thought, therefore, was that I might send a copy of *The Wealth of Nations* as an inaugural present to the next pope, whoever he might be.

William Rees-Mogg, *The Times*

Sideways is beautifully written, terrifically acted; it is paced and constructed with such understated mastery that it is a sort of miracle... Audiences at the screenings where I have been present may have heard something like a fusillade of gunshots from the auditorium; it was the sound of my heart breaking into a thousand pieces.

Peter Bradshaw, *The Guardian*

A friend told me about this vibrator in the shape of a tree with a snake wrapped round it that made you burst into tears when you had an orgasm. I did not believe it but I bought one and it worked.

Sam Roddick discusses her 'ethical erotica' business, *The Guardian*

Ricks smiles and says he gave up golf "when the Conservative party invaded Suez. It might not seem much of a gesture, but it mattered to me and I think it sent a pretty clear signal."

Profile of Christopher Ricks, *Guardian Review*

THE NEOPHILIACS

No it isn't and no they aren't

"Is Belgravia the new Beirut?"

Evening Standard

"Is Balham the new Notting Hill?"

Waitrose Food Illustrated

"Is separated the new engaged?"

Mail On Sunday

"Are laptops the new accordions?"

artsjournal.com

"Are deer the new mink?"

Shooting Times

"Are Don'ts the new Dos?"

Glamour magazine

"Are pets the new kids?"

Red magazine

"Are men the new women?"

"Is Gloucestershire the new Hollywood?"

"Is porridge the new sushi?"

"Are the British the new Germans?"

"Have you noticed that bottled water is the new hotel telephone?"

"Is bad the new good?"

"Are Wednesdays the new Sundays?"

"Are rental regulations the new speed cameras?"

"Is Google the new God?"

ON GUARD: A police officer keeps watch outside eurochange after the robbery   Picture: Hattie Miles

Bureau de change robbed at gunpoint

Bournemouth Daily Echo

Playtex said women had complained a strap connecting the two cups of the Deep Plunge Clearly Daring bra broke while it was being worn.

The company blamed tearing in fabric connecting the bra cups, and said "less than a handful" had been affected.

BBC News on Ceefax

RIÊU CÁ CHÉP

Crap in hot-pot
Crape dans la fondue

Bo Tung Xed restaurant,
Ho Chi Ming City

Animal smuggling in Australia is not all one way. Last month officers arrested a man trying to enter the country with a snake in his trousers.

The Times

LUVVIES

"I work away from home so much, I work in exile so much. British actors are a disapora unto themselves."

Sir Ben Kingsley, *Sunday Times*

What annoys you most about yourself?
"The fact that I am constantly striving for perfection and my inability to let go of my inner strength."

Anastacia, *The Independent Review*

"On the first day of shooting, after a couple of weeks of rehearsing, Natalie [Portman] brought Julia [Roberts] a little silver necklace with a word spelled out in the middle. The word was c**t. Julia was enchanted and loved it and said it was the sweetest present she'd ever had. Then, on the last day of shooting, she had a present for Natalie and it was a silver necklace and it spelled out 'Li'l C**t'. That's how free they are and what good friends they were."

Mike Nichols, *Evening Standard*

"I'm focusing more on playing the character of Widow Twankey, which I'm approaching in the same way I would any acting part. She's a complex character: a survivor who's been round the world, a north-of-England woman who's wound up raising her son in Peking and would do absolutely anything to protect him. That maternal urge is the strongest element of her character."

Ian McKellen, *The Guardian*

"I thought of Melrose Place as like Andy Warhol, and I think of this show as Kandinsky or Francis Bacon."

Marcia Cross, *Desperate Housewives*

The actor said, "It's absolutely integral to my whole career that I have the luxury of being eloquent and lucid in two languages.

"It allows me a metaphor to debate with myself.

"English actors often say they have Shakespeare, and that's another language. Well I have three: Shakespeare, English and Welsh."

Rhys Ifans, *The Daily Post*

"I do smaller films, though I will make a fourth Die Hard in 2006. We have a great script for that. I like to work; I want to work. Ben Kingsley said something that stuck with me. He said actors are like gladiators. No matter what, you put on the armor, go out to the arena and fight again."

Bruce Willis, *LA Times*

"Building a character is like constructing a cathedral. Actors are plonked onto the fringes of society, but we're crucial to the survival of the tribe because storytelling is one of the oldest activities. I think of acting as healing the audience, and for me, functioning the best I can allows me not to get sick, as it were."

Sir Ben Kingsley, *Radio Times*

"He [Peter O'Toole] taught me to pee," she cries, but does not go into detail, and I don't want to abuse her civil rights or my own by making her do so.

Saffron Burrows interviewed by
Jan Moir, *Daily Telegraph*

Fresh from playing the central character in the Bridget Jones novels, actress Renée Zellweger is to turn her own hand to writing. Zellweger, 33, said she planned to write "fiction, non-fiction, whatever I'm feeling when I pick up the pen".

Metro

"It uses up more of you emotionally, spiritually, physically, than any part I've encountered," Redgrave says. "It's like you set out in a boat that's only just seaworthy, which is your own body and understanding and so on, and you are picked up in this maelstrom and dashed against the rocks and battered to smithereens and little bits of you emerge as driftwood..."

Corin Redgrave, *The Times*

It's a **DUMB DUMB DUMB DUMB** world

Dumb America

Anne Robinson: Which island in the Indian Ocean was named after the date of its discovery, the 25th of December 1643?
Contestant *(after deep thought)*: Guam?

The Weakest Link

Presenter: Which former British Prime Minister provided a eulogy by video link at the funeral of Ronald Reagan?
Contestant: Winston Churchill.

Studio 7, The WB Network

Presenter: Which former British colony was handed back to the Chinese in 1997?
Contestant: London.

Studio 7, The WB Network

Anne Robinson: Which prison shipped out the last of its inmates and closed down in 1963?
Contestant: Australia.

The Weakest Link

Dumb Ireland

Tim Kelly: What birthday does a bicentennial celebrate?
Contestant: Er...
Kelly: I'll give you a hint. Centennial is one hundred and bi means two.
Contestant: 102?

Today FM, Dublin

Dumb Australia

DJ: Which country does Mexico share its largest border with?
Contestant: Pass.
DJ: I'll give you a clue. It's very big.
Contestant: Greece.

96FM Perth, WA

Dumb New Zealand

Presenter: What's another name for Cosa Nostra?
Contestant: Ummm... Amnesty International?

MoreFM, Christchurch, NZ

Dumb Wimbledon

Anne Robinson: What letter of the alphabet sounds exactly like the name of a female sheep?
Andy Roddick: Baa.

The Weakest Link

Pseuds Corner

Birth Announcements

FREEMAN-ATTWOOD – On February 12th, 2002, to Emmy, wife of Julian Freeman-Attwood, a daughter Lily Tibet, a sister for Ivy Antarctica.
Daily Telegraph

PITMAN – On March 18th, 2002, to ALLISON 'Pooee' (née Gubbins) and SPENCER, a beautiful daughter, Mimi Magenta Poodle.
Daily Telegraph

CREWE-READ – On October 21st, 2001, in London, to EMMA (née Garton) and DAVID, a son. Sacha John-Randulph Offley, a brother for Honey-Bee and half-brother for Caspian, Daniel and Gabriella. Direct descendant of Henry de Criwa c.1150 and Lord Crewe of Crewe.

Daily Telegraph

KEAYS Theodore John Briffa, October 2nd, 2003. Another naked apelet, sibling to Chunkfish and Mudslug and son to bemused parents. Hail.

The Guardian

CUDDEFORD de CLERMONT-TONNERRE – On Wednesday July 23rd, 2003, to HERMIONE and ALASTAIR, a daughter, Allegra Marie Rosenius Angel Belle Sydney.

Daily Telegraph

CHAPMAN – On Christmas Day, 2003, to Janette (née Cousins) and Richard, a daughter, Mistletoe Betty Berengaria, a darling sister for Thomas, Felicity and Araminta.

Daily Telegraph

PITMAN – On May 7th, 2004, to POOEE (née Gubbins) and SPENCER, a beautiful daughter, Ruby Rhapsody Panda, a sister for Mimi Magenta Poodle.

Daily Telegraph

Sudoku
classic

Fill in the grid so that every row,
every column and every 3x3 box
contains the numbers 1 to 9.
Gone wrong? Start again at:
guardian.co.uk/sudoku
Solution in Monday's paper,
left: solution 023
**Free tough puzzles at
www.puzzler.co.uk/guardian**

Grauniad